ETHICAL
LIVING™

—AN ETHICAL—

DIET

ERICA GREEN

Rosen
YA™

New York

Published in 2020 by The Rosen Publishing Group, Inc.
29 East 21st Street, New York, NY 10010

Library of Congress Cataloging-in-Publication Data

Names: Green, Erica, author.
Title: An ethical diet / Erica Green.
Description: First edition. | New York : Rosen Publishing, 2020.
| Series: Ethical living | Includes bibliographical references and index. | Audience: Grades 7–12.
Identifiers: LCCN 2017055569| ISBN 9781508180524 (library bound) | ISBN 9781508180531 (pbk.)
Subjects: LCSH: Vegetarianism—Juvenile literature. | Meat—Moral and ethical aspects—Juvenile literature. | Animal welfare—Juvenile literature.
Classification: LCC TX392 .G69 2019 | DDC 179/.3—dc23
LC record available at https://lccn.loc.gov/2017055569

Manufactured in the United States of America

CONTENTS

The first person to give a name to the idea of not eating animal flesh was Pythagoras of Samos (580 BCE), a Greek philosopher and mathematician. Pythagoras argued that it was wrong to kill or eat living creatures. His ideas influenced generations of thinkers, so much so that up until the early 1800s a meatless diet was called a Pythagorean diet. Meanwhile, followers of early Indian religions, such as Hinduism, Buddhism, and Jainism, developed religious arguments for not eating meat. Ancient authors argued that a plant-based diet is healthier for humans, that animals deserve justice, and that the ideal world is a nonviolent world. This idea of nonviolence, or nonharming, was represented in the Sanskrit word *ahimsa*.

In the early nineteenth century, in England and America, people who did not eat meat became known as vegetarians. The first Vegetarian Society was founded in England in 1847, followed by the American Vegetarian Society in 1850. The word "vegetarian" shares its roots with the word "vegetable," and would seem to indicate that all vegetarians followed a plant-based diet. In reality, as a newspaper pointed out in 1884, there were two kinds of vegetarians. More moderate vegetarians ate eggs, milk, or fish while more "extreme" vegetarians ate no animal products at all. Officially, the Vegetarian Society followed the moderate way, but members who took an ethical approach increasingly argued against consuming anything that came from animals.

One famous member of the Vegetarian Society was Mahatma Gandhi, leader of the Indian independence movement and a believer in nonviolence. Gandhi gave a speech to the society in 1931, arguing that people should become vegetarian for ethical reasons, not just for their health. Gandhi said that it was not right for humans to live on "fellow animals." A growing number of vegetarians agreed with him, and a few years later they formed a breakaway group— the vegans.

The founding document of veganism is a typewritten four-page newsletter with a hand-drawn masthead. This is the very first issue of the *Vegan News*, produced in 1944. Donald Watson, who wrote and typed up the newsletter, took the suggested name Allvegan and shortened it, stating, "The virtue of having a short title is best known to those of us who, as secretaries of vegetarian societies, have to type or write the word vegetarian thousands of times a year!"

More seriously, Watson stated that it had become increasingly clear that dairy production involved "much cruel exploitation and slaughter of highly sentient life," and that those members of the society who had been following a diet free from all animal food, and who wanted others to do the same, were ready to share

Gandhi's parents were vegetarian for religious reasons. Ghandi experimented with eating meat as a teenager but then made an ethical choice to stop eating meat or milk products.

their ideas and experiences. In answer to critics who said that the time was not right, Watson wrote, "Can time ever be ripe for any reform unless it is ripened by human determination?"

The vegan movement has grown many branches since the Vegan Society planted the original seed. But like the original ethical vegans, today's vegans are individuals who are determined, each day, to make cruelty-free choices based on the belief that the exploitation of animals by humans is wrong.

I AM VEGAN: FROM AWARENESS TO ACTION

The decision to form the Vegan Society was made by just six people, including Donald Watson and his wife, Dorothy. These six people were the first to say, "I am vegan." From this small beginning a movement grew, and the day the society was founded, November 1, is now celebrated as World Vegan Day.

The Vegan Society soon had a branch in the United States and in 1960 the American Vegan Society adopted the word ahimsa, or harmlessness, as their aim. In 1979, the original Vegan Society defined veganism as a way of living that "seeks to exclude—as far as is possible and practicable—all forms of exploitation of, and cruelty to, animals for food, clothing, or any other purpose; and by extension, promotes the development and use of animal-free alternatives for the benefit of humans, animals, and the environment."

CHOOSING VEGAN

The number of vegans is still small, but it is growing. According to a study by the *Vegetarian Times*, around one million Americans (0.5 percent of the population) called themselves vegan in 2008. By 2017, that number had grown to 6 percent. Many of those people are vegan for ethical reasons. At some moment in their lives, they woke up to the way humans treat animals and decided to act. There is no wrong time to do this—people make changes in their life when the time is right for them.

Ten-year-old vegan and animal rights activist Genesis Butler is featured in *The Invisible Vegan,* a documentary about health and wellness in the African-American community.

GENESIS BUTLER

For Genesis Butler, it was a "chicken nuggets" moment. Genesis stopped eating meat at age three after asking her mom where chicken nuggets came from. At first her mom said, "from the

8

store," but then had to admit, "we kill animals for them." A year later, she saw her mom nursing her baby sister and asked, "Mom, where does the milk I drink come from?" Learning that mother cows produced the milk to feed their own babies, Genesis decided she didn't want to take milk from the mouths of baby cows, so she stopped drinking milk and eating dairy products. By the age of nine, Genesis was an animal rights activist and ethical vegan, convincing her local council to support Meatless Mondays. At the age of ten, she gave a TEDx Talk and started a nonprofit foundation.

LAUREN ORNELAS

When Lauren Ornelas was growing up in Texas farmland in the 1970s, she had a terrible thought. What if the hamburger she ate was responsible for separating a cow from its family? Feeling bad for the cows, she gave up meat for a while, but it didn't stick. Then,

Lauren Ornelas founded the Food Empowerment Project to raise awareness about how making ethical food choices can help bring about positive change in the world.

in high school, Lauren learned about veganism and animal rights and decided that defending animals was her path in life. Later still, Ornelas realized it was not only animals that suffer to put food on our plates. Slaughterhouse workers and farm workers suffer, too. Other foods we love, such as chocolate, are sometimes produced by people who are mistreated. For Ornelas, her food choices led her to think about changing the world. Sadly, many people eat hamburgers without ever thinking about cows in a field—and most cows today do not even get to live in fields.

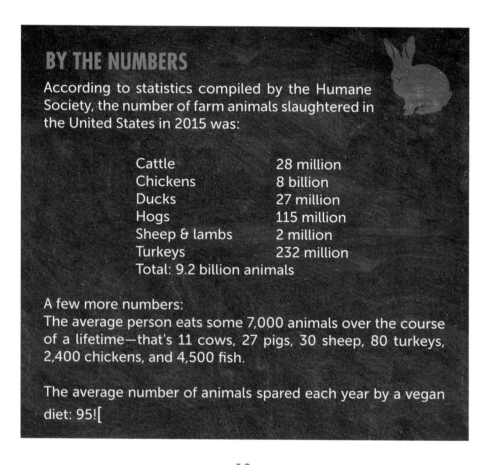

BY THE NUMBERS

According to statistics compiled by the Humane Society, the number of farm animals slaughtered in the United States in 2015 was:

Cattle	28 million
Chickens	8 billion
Ducks	27 million
Hogs	115 million
Sheep & lambs	2 million
Turkeys	232 million
Total: 9.2 billion animals	

A few more numbers:
The average person eats some 7,000 animals over the course of a lifetime—that's 11 cows, 27 pigs, 30 sheep, 80 turkeys, 2,400 chickens, and 4,500 fish.

The average number of animals spared each year by a vegan diet: 95![

THE ANIMALS WE USE FOR FOOD

Each year, around 70 billion farm animals are produced for food. In the United States, 98 percent of the animals raised for food are factory farmed. Factory farms, or concentrated animal feeding operations (CAFOs), raise animals as commodities to become the meat and animal products we buy in the store. Like humans and other animals, including the pets we love, every farmed animal is a sentient being that feels pain, values its own life, and will try to avoid death if it can. But farmed animals are born to be slaughtered, either for their meat or because they are no longer useful as milk-producing or egg-laying machines.

Trillions of aquatic animals are killed for food each year. Between 970 and 2,700 billion fish are caught in the wild. Many of these fish are used for fish oil or to make fishmeal to feed farmed fish. Meanwhile up to 120 billion farmed fish and over 400 billion crustaceans (crayfish, crabs, lobsters, prawns, and shrimp) are killed for food.

It is easy (although not fun) to learn about factory farming. There are many videos available online—*What Came Before* is a good place to start. Of course, you can become and stay a vegan without forcing yourself to look inside the slaughterhouse, but for many vegans, understanding the cruelty has helped them to commit to veganism. Others feel it is important to continue to bear witness, to take in the suffering without looking away.

GARY YOUROFSKY

For a surprising number of vegans younger than twenty-five, their path to veganism began with the words, "Today we're going to talk about the world's forgotten victims—animals." These words were spoken to Georgia Tech students in 2010 by activist and educator Gary Yourofsky, in a speech that was filmed and uploaded to the internet with the title, "Best Speech You Will Ever Hear." The speech has been watched over eleven million times.

Activist Gary Yourofsky has dedicated his life to being a voice for animals; he became a teacher so that he could talk to students about animal rights.

Yourofsky has described the moment he began thinking about how animals are treated. His stepfather took him behind the scenes at a circus and Yourofsky saw an elephant in chains. As Yourofsky tells it, "I looked into the elephant's eyes and all

I saw was sadness and despair." While still a meat eater, Yourofsky learned about the realities of the animal products industry by spending six weeks in a pig slaughterhouse. "I saw the pigs at the slaughterhouse, I knew I had to make a decision. Was I going to be their friend or their enemy?"

ANITA KRAJNC

When Anita Krajnc adopted her dog Mr. Bean, she began walking him past the pig slaughterhouse near where she lived in Toronto. Every day, she would watch as large trucks full of pigs pulled up outside the slaughterhouse. At the time, Krajnc was reading about men like Mahatma Gandhi and Leo Tolstoy, who took action in their local communities and influenced millions of people as a result. Krajnc decided to remind people about what was going on in the building, so she set up a group called Toronto Pig Save. The group began "bearing witness" to the pigs arriving for slaughter. One day, during a heat wave, the group filmed the overheated, thirsty pigs in the trucks. Then they began giving the pigs water. In 2015, Krajnc was arrested for giving water to a thirsty pig. For two years, while she waited to go to court, Anita Krajnc continued to show up and give water to the pigs. Many others did the same. Soon, there were more than 150 Save groups around the world.

During Krajnc's trial, Dr. Lori Marino was called to testify about pigs and personhood. She said that

a person is self-aware, has complex emotions, and is sentient. She said that under that definition, pigs are persons, not property. In the end, the judge disagreed. The law says that pigs are property. Krajnc hopes the law will change one day. As she says, what is legal and what is ethical are not always the same. "I was charged for an act of compassion … I wasn't worried, because I did the right thing." The

Activists Anita Krajnc (*left*) and Diane Warren (*right*) speak at a Humane Society event in 2016. "Kindness to all creatures is not an option but the only way," said Warren.

case highlighted the plight of the pigs and many people were affected by video of the pigs in the trucks. Many more Save groups were formed in other cities. In 2017, the case against Krajnc was dismissed. She continues to hold vigils and bear witness in Toronto.

TAKING THE PLUNGE

In a world full of alternatives, people in developed countries now choose, rather than need, to use animals for food. Vegans have decided that the only ethical food is food that is produced without harm to animals. By example and through activism they hope

KAREN'S TURKEY RESCUE

Karen Dawn is an animal welfare advocate and author of the book *Thanking the Monkey: Rethinking the Way We Treat Animals*. In 2000, Dawn visited a farm sanctuary and met Olivia, a turkey who had been rescued from a factory farm. Dawn fell in love with Olivia, and each year at Thanksgiving she put a photo of Olivia at the center of her table. Olivia has since died, but in her memory Dawn stages a yearly turkey rescue at Thanksgiving. She finds two live turkeys, takes them to her house, washes and blow-dries their feathers and has them as guests at her vegan dinner. After Thanksgiving, they go to the same farm sanctuary where Olivia lived out her days. As Dawn says, "It's a fun way to send a serious message about the lack of anti-cruelty standards for poultry."

to persuade others to make an ethical choice about the food on their plates.

Each day, one meal at a time, we can all choose to do less harm by making veganism part of our lives. So are you ready to take the plunge and find out how veganism works? It's easier than you think.

Chapter Two

EAT YOUR ETHICS: THE VEGAN SHOPPING LIST

Think about an animal that you care about—any animal. It might be your family dog, your two cats, your rabbit, or the fish in your fish tank. Then think about the fact that people eat, or have eaten, those animals. Think about the animals you have studied or watched on wildlife shows—animals with surprising intelligence, such as the octopus, animals that live a long time, like the turtle, or monkeys and apes that are so much like us. People eat, or have eaten, these animals. We think that the animals we choose to eat are different from the animals we love or the animals we admire and study. But they are all animals. We are all animals.

Vegans choose not to eat anything that comes from an animal—nothing with a face, feet, wings, or fins. If something from an animal source was used in the production of a product, vegans do not consume it. Vegans also avoid wearing leather, wool, silk, or feathers. If you are vegan, you do not eat meat, poultry, fish, eggs, dairy products, or honey and beeswax.

Here are some reasons why those things are not on the vegan shopping list.

LEAVE THESE OFF THE LIST

As much as possible, vegans abstain from any activity, food, business, or product that involves causing harm in any way to any living, sentient creatures. The methods we use to raise animals for meat, eggs, and dairy cause pain and suffering to those animals.

BEEF AND DAIRY FROM COWS

Cows and steers raised for beef are packed together in feedlots that hold thousands of animals. They are castrated, dehorned, and branded without painkillers.

Dairy cows, raised for their milk, spend much of their life in confinement as well. Twice a day (or more), they are hooked up to milking machines. Some are given a bovine growth hormone to boost their production of milk. To maintain milk flow, cows are kept almost constantly pregnant. The newborn calves are removed from their mothers directly after birth so that their mothers will keep on producing milk.

Most male calves are raised and slaughtered for beef. Some are kept in small crates for sixteen weeks to be killed for veal. Most female calves become part of the dairy herd. When a female cow's dairy production declines, it is also slaughtered for beef.

PORK, HAM, AND BACON FROM PIGS

Breeding sows are kept in metal crates so small they cannot turn around. They give birth to and nurse their litters of ten to twelve piglets in these crates. On top of that, the sow's usual nursing period of twelve weeks is cut to two to four weeks so the sows can be impregnated again. After three to four years, the mothers are sold and slaughtered.

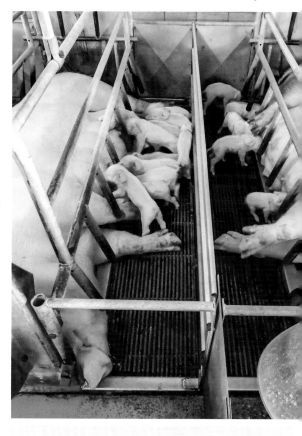

Farrowing crates, such as these, may make life safer for piglets, because the sow cannot roll over and crush them, but the sow suffers from having no room to move.

Approximately 20 percent of the prematurely weaned piglets die of stress and disease. The survivors are tagged, castrated without pain relief, and placed in stacked wire cage "nurseries" where they are fed a synthetic milk replacement (like baby formula). When able to eat solid food, the piglets are transferred to crowded pens, where they stay for six months, only to be slaughtered.

MEAT FROM CHICKENS

Chickens raised for meat are crowded into large sheds containing tens of thousands of birds. Bred to gain weight rapidly, many of these chickens are crippled by their own weight and find it too difficult to walk.

Over time, the sheds fill with toxic gases, such as hydrogen sulfide, ammonia, and methane. And after just seven weeks, the "adult" chickens are transported for slaughter.

EGGS FROM CHICKENS

Because the male chicks are not needed, they are separated out and killed. The female chicks have the tips of their beaks seared off with a hot iron to stop them from pecking other hens.

Egg-laying chickens are crammed into wire-mesh cages, with between five and seven birds squished into cages the size of a newspaper page, all stacked on top of one another. The birds are made to stand on sloping, wire-mesh floors, which cut their feet, while sharp walls rub off their feathers and bruise their skin.

When the birds are around fifteen months, they are moved into an area with lower lighting and fed a low-calorie diet for seven to fourteen days. This stresses their bodies and leads to increased egg production, which lasts for about another six months. Then, these birds are sent to slaughter.

FISH

Modern commercial fisheries deploy goliath ships, cutting-edge electronic equipment, and satellite technology to track the fish they're after. They are extremely efficient, killing hundreds of billions of aquatic animals annually—a far greater slaughter than in any other industry. As a result, 90 percent of the world's large fish populations have been wiped out in the past fifty years.

More than 30 percent of fish and other aquatic animals eaten each year are raised in aquafarms. Up

Environmentalists argue that aquafarms, such as this Russian salmon farm, are helping to poison the oceans by releasing diseases and parasites from overcrowded tanks into the surrounding waters.

to 40 percent of the fish in aquafarms die before the farmers can even kill them for food. Those who survive remain fully conscious yet unable to breathe as they start down the slaughter line, because fish slaughter plants in the United States are not compelled by law to stun them. Large fish, such as salmon, are sometimes cruelly bashed on the head with a wooden bat to make them more manageable. Many are seriously injured but still alert as they're being cut open.

HONEY

Honey is the regurgitation of the food bees eat. Bees make this food from the nectar of flowers and use it to feed their hive and their young. Each bee only makes a small amount of honey—a tablespoon of honey might be the life's work of up to 36 bees. To obtain honey, the bees are smoked out of their hives. Bees are likely to die every time honey, the comb, or beeswax is collected.

THE HIDDEN VICTIMS

Hundreds of thousands of wild animals (prairie dogs, coyotes, wolves, mountain lions, bears, and bison) are killed to stop them from interfering with agribusiness. Millions of starlings and blackbirds are poisoned each year to keep them away from animal feed. Wildlife is also threatened by habitat destruction. Animal agriculture turns hundreds of acres of forest, wetlands, and other habitats into land for animal feed crops and grazing.

The fishing industry also has hidden victims. Many fisheries around the world throw away more fish than they keep. For example, with shrimp fishers, up to six pounds of other species may be thrown away for every pound of shrimp. The unwanted or unsellable species that are thrown away, called bycatch, may include dolphins, turtles, and seabirds.

Plant-based food production may also have both animal and human victims. Palm oil is an edible oil that is used in margarine, shortening, cooking oil, soups, sauces, crackers, and other baked goods. To clear land for palm oil plantations, animals are removed, poached, and killed. In Indonesia, palm oil production has led to the deaths of many orangutans and other endangered species, such as Sumatran tigers, Sumatran rhinos, and Asian elephants. People are also displaced from their homes as the demand for palm oil grows.

WHAT'S ON THE VEGAN SHOPPING LIST?

Now that we know what vegans don't eat, let's look at what they do eat. The short answer is—everything else! The slightly longer answer is that if it comes from a plant, a vegan will eat it.

PLANT-BASED WHOLE FOODS

Vegans eat fruits, veggies, and herbs. They eat bread, pasta, oats, rice, and other grains of all kinds. They eat legumes, including soybeans, chickpeas, lentils,

HIDDEN ANIMAL INGREDIENTS

Many of the animal ingredients that are most likely to show up in processed food have names that disguise their animal origin:

Carmine is a red food coloring made from ground-up beetles.
Casein is a milk protein.
Collagen and keratin are rendered slaughterhouse proteins.
Gelatin is derived from the skins or bones of animals.
Glycerine, lactic acid, mono or **diglycerides**, and **stearic acid** can be produced from slaughterhouse fat (but also can be vegan).
Lactose is a sugar extracted from milk.
Lard and **tallow** are names for animal fat.
Whey is a milk-based by-product of cheese making.

navy beans, black beans, and split peas. They eat peanuts. They eat nuts, such as brazils, cashews, hazelnuts, and almonds. They eat sunflower, pumpkin, flax, and sesame seeds. They use oils that come from plants, such as olive, coconut, and canola.

VEGAN VERSIONS

Being a vegan does not mean eating only raw, unprocessed whole foods (although there are some vegans who eat that way.) There are many prepared and processed foods for vegans to eat, and that list is growing every day. Most dairy products, such as ice cream, yogurt, cheese, cream cheese, butter,

A vegan diet is anything but boring. Let the full rainbow spectrum of fruits and vegetables inspire you to make your meals and snacks fresh, colorful, and fun.

and milk, have a vegan version. Vegans replace animal flesh with fake or "faux" meat made of soy, seitan (from wheat gluten), and other plant proteins. Many vegans enjoy traditional soy products, such as tofu and tempeh. Vegan bakers have learned to use ground flax seed, apple sauce, or chia seeds in place of eggs.

TO B12 OR NOT TO B12

If you eat a variety of foods, including fruits and veggies of all colors, with plenty of beans and other

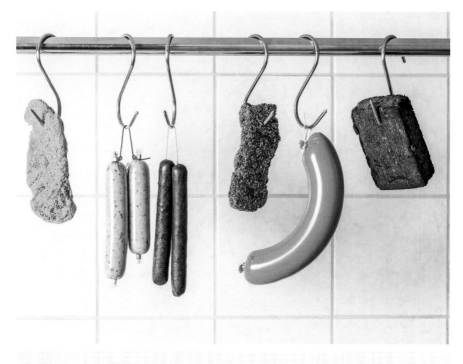

These days, there's no need for vegans to miss out on their deli favorites—these vegan sausages and other faux meat products look just like the real thing.

legumes and some good fats from nuts and seeds, you will be as healthy as your meat-and-dairy-eating friends. If they are junk-food junkies, you may even be healthier! There's just one vital nutrient that a plant-based diet doesn't have: vitamin B12. Animal products contain B12 because it comes from bacteria that live in the animal's intestines or on their food. Some foods that vegans eat, such as nutritional yeast and soy milk, are fortified with B12. But the safest way to make sure you get enough is to take a supplement. In other words, the answer is always yes to B12.

MYTHS AND FACTS

MYTH: It's hard to get enough protein on a plant-based diet.

FACT: Almost all Americans (including vegans) get more than enough protein. Plants such as beans and even many vegetables are a good source of protein.

MYTH: People become weak and frail on a vegan diet.

FACT: There are many successful vegan athletes including tennis champions Venus and Serena Williams, NFL player David Carter, ultra-athlete Rich Roll, and many more.

MYTH: Only rich people can go vegan—it's just too expensive.

FACT: Staples such as grains, potatoes, bananas, and beans are some of the cheapest (and healthiest) things you can buy in the supermarket.

Chapter Three

VEGAN CHOICES: BALANCING YOUR MEALS AND YOUR LIFE

In the United States, around 6 percent of the population is vegan. That means that 94 percent of the population is not. If you are a vegan, you will most likely be the only vegan in your family. You may be the only vegan in your circle of friends. There may be some—but not many—vegans at your school. All vegans have to find a way to eat with (and get along with) other people, while at the same time sticking to their principles and eating in a way that does not cause harm to others.

One way that many vegans take control of what they eat is by learning how to cook. That way, they know what they are eating. And it doesn't have to be complicated. There are many vegan food blogs and vegan cookbooks. If you are a new vegan, check Facebook, YouTube, and Instagram, find a food blog you like, or check out a cookbook from the library and start experimenting.

IN THE FAMILY KITCHEN

Sharing a kitchen with a house full of people who love meat and dairy may have its challenges. If you are vegan, you might want to claim your own part of the refrigerator or your own shelf in the kitchen. That way, whoever is making food in the kitchen knows where the vegan-friendly foods are. Ask to add more seasonal fruits and veggies to the family shopping list. Offer to prepare a large fruit salad or a salad with vegan dressing as a side dish for family meals and special occasions. Anybody with a bit of patience and some chopping skills can become a salad ninja!

Take charge of the refrigerator and add some labels to let family or roommates know where they can find the vegan foods.

START THE DAY RIGHT

Breakfast is a good place to start when it comes to preparing your own meals. Smoothies and overnight oats are basics that you can adapt to include the flavors and textures you like. To make overnight oats, put oats in a jar or container and stir in water or a plant-based milk, such as soy or oatmeal. Add fruit, nuts, maple syrup, cinnamon, and whatever else you fancy. Then place in the refrigerator overnight.

For a breakfast smoothie, blend together plant-based milk (or water) and fruit, such as a banana or frozen berries. Add some protein powder and flax seeds for extra goodness. If you prefer a heartier breakfast, find a recipe for tofu scramble and add some vegan 'fake' bacon or cook up some meaty mushrooms.

PACK A LUNCH

Chances are, your school cafeteria offers animal-free options, such as salads, veggie sides, and veggie burgers. If they don't offer many plant-based foods, you could try suggesting foods you'd like to see them serve. In the meantime, a good way to make sure you are eating a balanced lunch is to prepare a sandwich or wrap containing lots of veggies and some plant-based protein.

To build your own sandwich or wrap, start with whatever bread you like, such as whole-grain, pita, lavash, or a wrap, tortilla, or bagel. Add some protein

Packing a vegan lunch box puts you in charge of the food you eat when you are away from home. Include nutritious plant-based foods and some vegan snack options.

in the form of nut butter, hummus, baked tofu, falafel, refried beans, or 'faux' meat or cheese. Add any veggies you like, either cooked or raw, including pickles, olives, and sprouts. Then add dressing, which could be a vegan mayo or a spread, such as guacamole, tahini, or chutney.

There's no need to limit yourself to sandwiches. Pack a salad, with a base of beans, roasted veggies, or even pasta. Leftover veggies and rice from the night before with a sauce, such as peanut or sweet chili, can be quite tasty. On cold days, take a thermos of hot soup.

DINNER TABLE CHALLENGES

If you eat dinner at home with your parents or other guardians, you may not have much control over what is served up. Even if you are learning to cook some vegan meals, you may not want to cook for yourself

DON'T FORGET TO SNACK!

To keep you going between meals, there are many great vegan snack options. These include:
- sliced fresh fruit or a handful of dried fruit
- nuts and seeds
- raw veggies and hummus
- celery with peanut butter
- crackers with nut butter
- vegan energy bars (brands include Clif and Luna)
- veggie or fruit crisps
- tortilla chips and salsa or guacamole
- nondairy yogurt
- vegan cookies
- microwave bean burrito

every night. Try asking the person doing the cooking to "veganize" some regular recipes. Veganizing involves swapping out vegan for nonvegan ingredients in standard dishes. For example, using vegetable broth rather than meat stock to cook soups and risottos, preparing vegetables with olive oil rather than butter, or using vegan mayo instead of egg mayo.

Why not ask the person who is cooking to keep the meat on the side where possible, or add some nonmeat side dishes? You can then substitute a plant-based protein. Finally, how about offering to cook your family a Meatless Monday meal? Try working on a vegan "signature dish" such as a really great marinara sauce. Your family of dedicated carnivores may not notice the meat is missing.

BEING A FOOD EVANGELIST

Support your favorite vegan food discovery, whether it is a recipe, a new ingredient, or a new vegan version of your favorite snack food. Model the good behavior you would like to see others follow by promoting products that are doing good and withholding support for those products that are doing bad. It is far better to rave to your friends about a new salted caramel coconut "nice cream" than to try to guilt them about the beef in their burger. You may not be able to spoon-feed them veganism, but you can literally spoon-feed them good plant-based ice cream! Every little bit helps.

VEGAN TO GO

It can be both exciting and challenging to eat out as a vegan. If you live in a major city, you are bound to notice new vegan food outlets popping up everywhere. Outside of urban centers, you might have to work harder to find a vegan place where you can go out to eat with friends and family. Fortunately, there's an app for that! The HappyCow app will show you where to find vegan food, wherever you are in the world.

Wherever you are as a vegan—at the mall, at the movies, in a pizza place—you may need to speak up about what you don't eat. Not everybody understands what a vegan is, so it's best to spell it out: no meat, no fish, no dairy, no honey. If your family are heading out to a restaurant for a special occasion, why not get someone to call ahead and ask what the vegan

options are? Most places are happy to help if they have some advance notice.

If you and your friends are ordering takeout pizza, check the menu online. If there is no vegan option, mix and match the toppings to get what you want. Some types of ethnic food are great for vegans. Middle Eastern food, with its hummus, falafel, and tahini sauce, is always good. Mexican outlets are also often vegan friendly—just check whether anything has been cooked in lard. These days, there are many creative veggie burgers out there—make it your mission to try them all!

If you find a great new vegan food outlet, or an old favorite that offers some great vegan options, make sure you support them by leaving an online review. At the same time, make the choice not to support places and products that harm animals to feed people.

These days, many dining establishments offer vegan options; keep an eye out for vegan and vegetarian eateries in your area.

Chapter Four

SPEAKING YOUR VEGAN TRUTH: CHECK YOUR FACTS, AVOID THE EXTREMES

O nce you've been vegan for a while and have worked out what to eat, use, and wear, you might decide you want to take your veganism to the next level. After all, the idea of ahimsa is not just to do the least harm, but to actively do the most good. That could mean making a change for the better at your school or within your community. It could mean telling others about veganism or about specific examples of animal cruelty. It might mean starting a YouTube channel or Instagram feed to inspire others. But before you begin talking to others about veganism, particularly about food, make sure you are as informed as you can be.

GETTING THE FACTS RIGHT

If you type "vegan" into a search engine you will soon see that everybody has an idea, an opinion, or an argument for or against veganism. You will also see that everybody these days is a nutritionist (or pretending to be one). And everything is a diet. Also, some vegans eat sugar, and some don't—why is that?

VEGANS AND SUGAR

If you are vegan, there are questions to be asked about how sugar is produced. Some sugar is filtered using bone char, also known as natural carbon. Bone char is made from the bones of slaughtered animals and is therefore not cruelty free. However, not all sugar is filtered with bone char.

A good place to find more detailed information on the question of sugar is the PETA (People for the Ethical Treatment of Animals) website. There you will learn that sugar is typically made from sugarcane, sugar beets, or coconuts. Beet and coconut sugar are never processed with bone char. Nor is organic sugar. But bone char is used to produce some sugar from sugarcane. PETA provides a list of companies that do not filter with bone char as well as a list of vegan-friendly sweeteners.

PETA urges that it is important to be informed about

Refined white sugar such as this is not always vegan. As an alternative, many vegans use sweeteners such as maple syrup, coconut sugar, or stevia.

sugar when buying or cooking with it. At the same time, being vegan doesn't have to mean being perfect. PETA encourages vegans not to get too stressed if they are unsure about the origin of sugar in a prepared food item. In other words, read the label, but don't give your best friend the third degree if she baked you vegan brownies but forgot to check the origin of the sugar.

JUNK SCIENCE

There is a lot of nutritional junk science and bad information on the internet. An example of junk science would be a study that draws all of its conclusions from one small study. For example, if ten people ate a mushroom-only diet for ten days, even under laboratory conditions, the results would not provide enough information to make a decision about whether the mushroom diet was a good idea. An example of bad information might be a website set

A plan plate such as this one helps with meal planning by showing the food choices and portion sizes that make up a balanced vegan meal.

up to promote the mushroom diet, sponsored by the Mushroom Institute, and given the seal of approval by the MI's official spokesperson, Dr. Julius Fungi.

When you have questions about nutrition, try to find the answers on a reputable website and check the qualifications of the person giving advice. Somebody like Ginny Messina, the Vegan RD (the RD stands for Registered Dietitian), at www.veganrd.com is an example of a reputable source of information. Look for the plant plate on her site, which packs a lot of information into a small space. It's probably best not to rely solely on your favorite YouTube vegan for nutritional information. Just because a vegan vlogger recommends eating ten bananas for breakfast doesn't mean you should do it. It may not even be ethical, depending on where the bananas have been sourced!

GOING TO EXTREMES

In life, as on YouTube, drama gets views and extreme diets capture attention. Three types of diets you may come across are Totally Raw, Low-Carb High-Fat, and Plant-Based Low-Fat. The problem is, they are what they sound like: diets. People follow these food plans specifically to lose weight. Ethical veganism, on the other hand, is a way of living. "Vegan" signifies only what you don't eat, it doesn't define you by what you do eat. A totally raw diet is a fad. Follow a fully raw vlogger for long enough and it's likely they will change or abandon their diet because it is not sustainable. Even people who become vegans for dietary reasons often stop being vegan. The ones who are more likely to make it a permanent lifestyle are the ethical vegans.

CONSIDER THE BANANA

Some food production may not harm animals, but may be cruel to humans and harm the environment. Take bananas, for example. The Food Empowerment Project's report, *Peeling Back the Truth on Bananas*, outlines some of the hidden cruelty of banana production. Workers on banana plantations often live in poor conditions and receive low wages. Children may work twelve-hour days and be exposed to chemicals. Deforestation may occur in order to plant more bananas. At the same time, bananas are a reasonably priced fruit that contains many beneficial nutrients.

The Food Empowerment Project (FEP) informs people about small, ethical producers of cruelty-free bananas. But ethical bananas are not available all over the United States. Organic bananas may be a good option, as they are not grown using chemicals, but workers may still have been paid very low wages—and organic bananas cost

When shopping for bananas, choose Fairtrade or cruelty-free bananas from an ethical source if possible. There is still work to be done to make this option available to everyone.

more. When weighing up the issue of bananas, FEP admits, "Bananas are tough!"

BEING A VEGAN ADVOCATE

So, you're ready to showcase your veganism. Many vegans do this by posting vegan-themed items on Facebook, inspirational "What I Eat in a Day" videos on YouTube, or artful photos of their vegan cuisine on Instagram. Some perform the valuable service of taste-testing every new vegan snack or flavor of vegan ice cream (somebody has to do it). Others

Vegan vloggers are helping to spread the vegan word online by showcasing the foods and recipes they love and offering advice for new vegans.

conduct vegan experiments, such as eating vegan while spending just one dollar per meal on food. They showcase the fact that a few simple ingredients— such as beans, rice, bananas, frozen veggies, and peanut butter—can be combined into surprisingly good meals. This helps to show people that they can eat vegan on a budget.

To be an effective advocate for veganism, share something specific such as a problem you solved. Perhaps you are an athlete and want to showcase the protein smoothies you make when you're in training. Perhaps you have a nut allergy and can share tips with other vegans. Maybe you want to try new vegan foods and blog your findings. One piece of advice, though: whatever you do, don't try eating only mush-rooms for a month.

10 GREAT QUESTIONS TO ASK A DIETITIAN

1. When I tell people I'm vegan, they say I won't be able to get enough protein from plants. Every time! How much protein do I need per day?

2. What are good fats and why are they good? What are the plant sources of good fats?

3. I'm not sure about soy—some people say it's bad. Should I avoid it?

4. What has more calcium, cow's milk or kale?

5. I've heard we need to eat fish or sea vegetables for iodine. Are there plant sources?

6. My mom says I need red meat for iron. Am I at risk of anemia if I don't eat red meat?

7. What is choline? Do I need it, and what foods is it found in?

8. What is nutritional yeast (or nooch) and why is it so nutritional?

9. Sometimes I live on PBJs. Are PBJs a good source of protein?

10. I have heard that Oreo cookies are vegan. Is that true?

Chapter Five

ANIMALS, PEOPLE, PLANET: TOWARD A COMPASSIONATE FUTURE FOR ALL

W hat if the world went vegan? One group of researchers in the UK tried to answer that question. Let's look at what they found and explore what their ideas might mean.

VEGAN BY 2050?

Researcher (and vegan) Dr. Marco Springmann led a team of researchers from the Oxford Martin School. The team built computer models to show what would happen if the world adopted different ways of eating, including a vegetarian and a vegan diet. One of their findings was that the widespread adoption of a vegan diet could cut greenhouse gas emissions by two thirds and save eight million lives by 2050.

In an interview with the newspaper *Oxford Today*, Springmann said that what we eat "greatly influences our personal health and the global environment." He

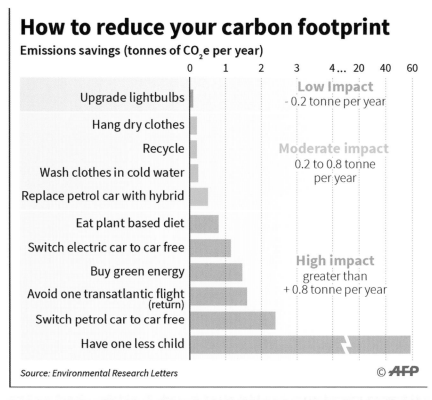

How to reduce your carbon footprint

Emissions savings (tonnes of CO_2e per year)

Upgrade lightbulbs	**Low Impact** - 0.2 tonne per year
Hang dry clothes	
Recycle	**Moderate impact** 0.2 to 0.8 tonne per year
Wash clothes in cold water	
Replace petrol car with hybrid	
Eat plant based diet	
Switch electric car to car free	
Buy green energy	**High impact** greater than + 0.8 tonne per year
Avoid one transatlantic flight (return)	
Switch petrol car to car free	
Have one less child	

0   1   2   3   4... 20   40   60

Source: Environmental Research Letters © **AFP**

Being vegan and eating a plant-based diet not only saves animals from a cruel death, it lowers your carbon footprint and helps in the fight against global warming.

said that the worst diets for health were those that had too much meat and not enough vegetables. He also said that our current food system is responsible for more than a quarter of all greenhouse gas emissions. That makes it a major cause of climate change.

Springmann grew up in Germany and changed to a plant-based diet while studying in the United States. Convinced by research showing that a vegan diet would be healthier, he began researching veganism in his own work. Springmann says that when he became a vegan he had to change how he shopped and ate. "Every day I was in the kitchen experimenting with different dishes. It was great." He also said that he did not miss meat and dairy. "I'm a researcher. If you give me some good studies, I try to change my behavior based on it."

Recent studies show that people should eat up to ten portions of fruit and vegetables a day to prevent an early death. Research from Oxford shows that vegans usually eat two to three more servings of fruit a day than meat eaters. Springmann points out that not only is a meat-based diet less healthy, but meat is bad for the environment, too. Other experts agree. Studies such as the 2006 UN report, *Livestock's Long Shadow*, show that meat production is responsible for the largest percentage of food-related greenhouse gas emissions, almost as large as from transport, such as cars and planes. In the United States, for example, an average family of four emits more greenhouse gases because of the meat they eat than from driving two cars. Most food-related emissions are caused by the methane that cows produce and by the large-scale growth of animal feed, which leads to deforestation.

Scientists warn that to prevent dangerous levels of climate change, we need to limit global warming to below a rise of two degrees Celsius. Yet Springmann's research shows just how difficult that will be. If the world continues to eat more meat, population

growth continues, and people in developing countries aspire to eat as much meat as people in the United States, then we will be headed for environmental crisis. "Things cannot stay the same," warns Springmann.

A WORLD WITHOUT MEAT

Some might say that a vegan doctor arguing that everybody should be vegan is not much different to Dr. Fungi advising everyone to live on mushrooms. So, what could go wrong if the world were vegan by 2050? Both the benefits and the potential problems were explored in a BBC documentary, *What Would Happen if the World Suddenly Went Vegetarian*?

THE BENEFITS OF TURNING AWAY FROM MEAT

As shown in the Oxford research, food-related emissions would drop by around 60 percent if people no longer ate red meat from methane-producing livestock. And if former pastures were turned back into forests and habitats for wild animals, that would help to slow down climate change and increase biodiversity. Large herbivores such as buffalo and carnivores such as wolves could return to the land, having been pushed out or killed so that people could raise cattle.

One-third of the land currently planted in crops is used to produce food for livestock. If animals were no longer raised for meat, up to 20 percent of pasture land could be used for growing more crops for people to eat.

Meanwhile, people would live longer and save money on medical bills without meat in their diet.

POTENTIAL PROBLEMS

As workers were displaced from the livestock industry, new jobs would need to be created and people would need to be retrained. New jobs might be created in agriculture, reforestation, or producing bioenergy. However, if those new jobs did not appear, there could be mass unemployment

While wild bison today are mostly found in national parks such as Custer State Park in South Dakota, it is possible that more populations could return if people no longer ate red meat.

and social problems. These problems could be particularly devastating for farming communities.

Without meat, many celebrations and traditions would disappear. History, family traditions, and national cultures would be changed or lost. There would be no more Thanksgiving turkey, no meat-based Christmas feast, game-day BBQ, or family chicken recipe cooked every year in remembrance. Communities around the world that give gifts of livestock at weddings and celebrations would also lose these traditions.

The disappearance of livestock such as sheep could change the land and have an impact on biodiversity.

However, where grazing animals have helped the land stay the same for centuries, some farmers could be paid to keep animals in order to protect the environment.

Finally, meat would need to be replaced with nutritious substitutes. Although a well-balanced vegan diet has been shown to be very healthy for humans, it is still the case that animal products contain more nutrients per calorie than staples like grains and rice. Choosing the right food to replace meat would be important to prevent a health crisis in the developing world, where there are already more than two billion undernourished people.

THE PLANTS ARE TAKING OVER

Lately, there has been an explosion of plant-based food products. Leonardo DiCaprio has invested in Beyond Meat, a plant-based burger. Dairy-free cheese may soon be better than the original. Dairy-free desserts, dairy-free yogurt, vegan fast food—there are new brands and better products every day. Soon people who love food will be asking their vegan friends for food tips!

Of course, all of these new products cost a lot more than simple vegan staples like beans and rice. It may take years for them to become as cheap and widely available as traditional plant-based products, such as soy milk or tofu. But for now, they are a taste of the future.

The country with the largest number of new vegan food products is, surprisingly, Germany. Companies have created plant-based versions of the foods that

MEAT WITHOUT ANIMALS?

Ryan Bethencourt is a vegan. His company, Indie-Tech, funds businesses that are trying to change the way food is produced, such as Memphis Meats, which created the world's first lab-grown meatball in 2016 (and then went on to create lab-grown chicken and duck). To produce the meat, tiny cells were taken from an animal and fed nutrients in the lab. Meat like this could be produced without needing to raise and kill the animals. Right now, lab-grown meat is very expensive, but the industry aims to offer affordable choices by 2021. Products like this may help reduce meat's environmental impact and go a long way toward ending cruelty to animals.

This burger was created with cells taken from a living cow. While this beef patty cost $325,000 to produce in 2013, the price tag has since been smashed, with $12 producing a single burger's worth of lab-grown meat in 2015—but it's still not close to being ready for public consumption.

are staples in the German diet, such as bratwurst and schnitzel. These are products that were traditionally made from veal, beef, or pork. The veganized versions are made of plant proteins, such as soy, wheat,

or tofu, which are woven and glued together to help create the texture and consistency of meat.

Not everybody thinks that such processed products are a good thing. Mock meats can be almost pure protein and need to be served with plenty of whole foods to provide a balanced diet. In general, processed foods may also be high in added salt and fat, and sometimes sugar, too.

WE ANIMALS

In a photo by Jo-Anne McArthur, a pig stares out through a small metal opening on the side of a truck. McArthur took the photo at a Toronto Pig Save vigil. McArthur has traveled the world to take pictures of animals—in slaughterhouses, zoos, and aquariums, in research labs, markets, and on farms. Many of her pictures are of things people prefer not to see, but McArthur also has photos of animals with their rescuers at shelters and sanctuaries. Like Anita Krajnc, when she gave water to thirsty pigs and was arrested for it, McArthur bears witness to what we do to animals. She does what she can. The pig in the truck was not saved, but the work goes on.

Jo-Anne McArthur's photographs are collected in a book called *We Animals*. She says that she was thinking about the words "you animal" and how we use them. Those words describe someone who is cruel, unclean, lesser, or unfit for human society. "What about *we* animals?" she asked herself. She dedicates her work to the fact that we're all animals: sentient beings with a will and desire to live free from harm and fear. McArthur became vegan in 2003 while working at Farm Sanctuary. All workers and volunteers had to be vegan while they were working there, out of respect for the animals. She has remained vegan. As she said in an "Ask Me Anything" post online, "For me veganism is not a deprivation but a joy!" Donald Watson would be proud.

Jo-Anne McArthur took this photograph for her *We Animals* project. Jane the pig is enjoying life at Farm Sanctuary, in New York, safe from being used for food.

Today, more and more people are leaving the meat off their plates and seeking out ethical, plant-based alternatives. Every time you choose a meal without animal products, you make an ethical choice. Every time someone chooses not to purchase a product containing palm oil, they act in favor of people and animals, and against deforestation and death. Every person who chooses to be vegan chooses kindness over cruelty, planet over profit, and health over harm. Every day, every meal, it's your choice. Choose wisely.

GLOSSARY

activism The use of direct and noticeable action to bring about political or social change.

agribusiness The business or industry of farming or agriculture; farming thought of as a large business.

ahimsa The principle of nonviolence toward all living beings; a philosophy of not harming others in thought, word, or action.

biodiversity The number of different species of plants and animals in an environment.

bycatch The unwanted fish and other marine creatures trapped by commercial fishing nets during fishing for a different species.

carnivore An organism that eats animal flesh.

climate change A long-term change in the Earth's weather patterns, especially a change due to an increase in atmospheric temperature.

commodity A raw material or primary agricultural product that can be bought and sold, such as milk, beef, pork, or chicken.

compassion The emotional and sympathetic awareness of another's suffering, combined with the motivation and desire to alleviate that suffering.

cruelty Inflicting pain or suffering by mistreatment or neglect.

deforestation The cutting down of trees in a large area, or the destruction of forests by people.

ethics The discipline dealing with what is good and bad and with moral duty and obligation; also, a set of moral principles governing an individual or a group.

exploitation The act of using resources or the act of treating people unfairly in order to benefit from their efforts or labor.

greenhouse gases Any gases, such as carbon dioxide, that trap heat in the atmosphere and contribute to the greenhouse effect.

herbivore An organism that exclusively eats plants.

methane A gas produced by the breaking down of organic matter.

nutrient A substance that provides nourishment essential for the maintenance of life and for growth.

omnivore An organism that eats a variety of foods of both plant and animal origin.

sentient A living being that is able to experience sensations, to feel and sense things.

vegan A strict vegetarian who does not eat any food that comes from animals (such as meat, eggs, dairy products, honey, and animal by-products, such as gelatin) and does not use any animal products (such as leather).

vegetarian A person who does not eat animal flesh, such as meat or fish, but who may eat eggs and/or dairy products.

FOR MORE INFORMATION

A Well-Fed World
3936 S Semoran Boulevard, #271
Orlando, FL 32822
(202) 495-1348
Website: http://awfw.org
Facebook and Twitter: @awellfedworld
A Well-Fed World is a hunger relief and animal pro-
   tection organization. They produce informational
   handouts on topics such as global hunger and
   global warming, as well as guides for going vegan.

Canadian Coalition for Farm Animals
131 Bloor Street West, Suite 200/140
Toronto, ON M5S 1R8
Canada
(416) 920-4984
Website: http://www.humanefood.ca
Facebook: @canadiancoalitionforfarmanimals
The Canadian Coalition for Farm Animals produces
   many resources including reports on the welfare
   of animals raised for food in Canada, brochures,
   postcards, and a newsletter.

Earthsave Canada
422 Richards Street #170
Vancouver, BC V6B 2Z4
Canada

(604) 731-5885
Website: http://www.earthsave.ca
Facebook and Twitter: @earthsavecanada
Earthsave Canada provides a directory of vegan and
veg-friendly restaurants, food trucks, and food
retailers along with resources, such as brochures.

Farm Sanctuary
3100 Aikens Road
Watkins Glen, NY 14891
(607) 583-2225
Website: http://www.farmsanctuary.org
Facebook and Twitter: @farmsanctuary
Farm Sanctuary provides many educational resources
including brochures on factory farming, guides to
becoming vegetarian or vegan, recipe booklets, and
research reports.

Mercy for Animals
8033 Sunset Boulevard, Suite 864
Los Angeles, CA 90046
(866) 632-6446
Website: http://www.mercyforanimals.org
Facebook and Twitter: @mercyforanimals
Mercy for Animals produces videos about factory
farming and vegan eating and as well as providing
personal support and coaching to new vegans.

Vegan Outreach
PO Box 1916

Davis, CA 95617
Website: http://veganoutreach.org
Facebook and Twitter: @veganoutreach
Vegan Outreach produces informational booklets and
    offers a humane educational program for schools.
    They also offer an email mentoring program for
    new vegans.

Vegetarian Resource Group
PO Box 1463
Baltimore, MD 21203
(410) 366-8343
Website: http://www.vrg.org
Facebook: @thevegetarianresourcegroup
Twitter: @vegresourcegrp
The Vegetarian Resource Group provides brochures,
    handouts, and resources by dietitians, such as *My
    Vegan Plate*. They also conduct polls and publish
    poll results on vegan and vegetarian topics.

FOR FURTHER READING

Bell, Heather, and Jenny Engel. *Vegan 101: A Vegan Cookbook: Learn to Cook Plant-Based Meals That Satisfy Everyone*. Berkeley, CA: Sonoma Press, 2016.

Brown, Jenny. *The Lucky Ones: My Passionate Fight for Farm Animals*. New York, NY: Avery, 2013.

Francione, Gary L., and Anna Charlton. *Eat Like You Care: An Examination of the Morality of Eating Animals*. Warsaw, Poland: Exempla Press, 2013.

Davis, Brenda, and Melina Vesanto. *Becoming Vegan: The Everyday Guide to Plant-Based Nutrition*. Summertown, TN: Book Publishing Company, 2013.

Frazier, Matt, and Matt Ruscigno. *No-Meat Athlete: Run on Plants and Discover Your Fittest, Happiest Self*. Beverley, MA: Fair Winds Press, 2013.

Freston, Kathy. *The Book of Veganish: The Ultimate Guide to Easing into a Plant-Based, Cruelty-Free, Awesomely Delicious Way to Eat, with 70 Easy Recipes Anyone Can Make*. New York, NY: Pam Krauss Press/Avery, 2016.

Harper, A. Breeze. *Sistah Vegan: Black Female Vegans Speak on Food, Identity, Health, and Society*. Brooklyn, NY: Lantern Books, 2010.

Jenkins, Steve, and Derek Walter. *Esther the Wonder Pig: Changing the World One Heart at a Time*. New York, NY: Grand Central Publishing, 2016.

McArthur, Jo-Anne. *We Animals.* Brooklyn, NY: Lantern Books, 2014.

Proctor, Reuben, and Lars Thomsen. *Veganissimo A to Z: A Comprehensive Guide to Identifying and Avoiding Ingredients of Animal Origin in Everyday Products.* New York, NY: The Experiment, 2013.

Rose, Marla. *The Adventures of Vivian Sharpe, Vegan Superhero.* Createspace, 2012.

Runkle, Nathan, and Gene Stone. *Mercy for Animals: One Man's Quest to Inspire Compassion and Improve the Lives of Farm Animals.* New York, NY: Avery, 2017.

Stewart, Tracey. *Do Unto Animals: A Friendly Guide to How Animals Live, and How We Can Make Their Lives Better.* New York, NY: Artisan Books, 2015.

Taft, Casey. Millennial Vegan: *Tips for Navigating Relationships, Wellness, and Everyday Life as a Young Animal Advocate.* Danvers, MA: Vegan Publishers, 2017.

Turner, Christie. *But I Could Never Go Vegan!: 125 Recipes That Prove You Can Live Without Cheese, It's Not All Rabbit Food, and Your Friends Will Still Come Over for Dinner.* New York, NY: The Experiment, 2014.

BIBLIOGRAPHY

Adaptt. "Profiles of Gary Yourofsky." Retrieved November 12, 2017. http://www.adaptt.org/about/news--profiles-of-gary-yourofsky.html.

Animal Voices Radio. "Bearing Witness with the Toronto Pig Save." Retrieved November 14, 2017. https://animalvoices.ca/2011/11/15/bearing-witness-with-the-toronto-pig-save.

A Well-Fed World. "Factory Farms." Retrieved November 2017. http://awfw.org/factory-farms.

Bennett, Beverly Lynn, and Ray Sammartano. *The Complete Idiot's Guide to Vegan Living*. New York, NY: Alpha Books, 2012.

Business Wire. "Top Trends in Prepared Foods 2017." Retrieved November 12, 2017. http://www.businesswire.com.

Card, John. "Lab-Grown Food." *The Guardian*, July 24, 2017. https://www.theguardian.com/small-business-network/2017/jul/24/lab-grown-food-indiebio-artificial-intelligence-walmart-vegetarian.

CrashCourse, January 16, 2017. "Non-Human Animals: Crash Course Philosophy #42." https://www.youtube.com/watch?v=y3-BX-jN_Ac&feature=youtu.be.

Eugene Veg Education Network. "EVEN Interview with lauren Ornelas." March 2016. http://www.all-creatures.org/articles/even-lauren-ornelas.html.

FEP. "Peeling Back the Truth on Bananas." Retrieved November 16, 2017. http://www.foodispower.org /bananas.

Gordon, Olivia. "What If We All Turned Vegan by 2050?" *Oxford Today*, March 11, 2017. http://www .oxfordtoday.ox.ac.uk/interviews/what-if-we-all -turned-vegan-2050#.

Hawthorne, Mark. *A Vegan Ethic: Embracing a Life of Compassion Toward All*. Winchester, UK: Change-makers Books, 2016.

Hall, Carla. "Obama's Pardoned Turkeys Aren't the Only Ones Deserving of a More Humane Thanksgiving." *LA Times*, November 26, 2017. http://www.latimes.com/opinion/opinion-la/la-ol -obama-pardon-turkeys-humane-20141126-story .html.

Messina, Ginny Kisch. The Vegan RD. Retrieved November 12, 2017. http://www.theveganrd.com /about.

Nuwer, Rachel. "What Would Happen If the World Suddenly Went Vegetarian?" BBC Future, September 27, 2016. http://www.bbc.com/future/story /20160926-what-would-happen-if-the-world -suddenly-went-vegetarian.

PETA. "Is Sugar Vegan?" Retrieved November 16, 2017. https://www.peta.org/living/food/is-sugar-vegan.

Pevreall, Katie. "10-Year-Old Genesis Butler Inspires Veganism at TEDx Talk in California." LiveKindly, May 2017. https://www.livekindly.co/genesis -butler-inspires-veganism-tedx-talk.

Senthilingam, Meera. "Are Germans Leading a Vegan Revolution?" CNN, July 31, 2017. http://edition .cnn.com/2017/05/03/health/germany-vegan -vegetarian-diets/index.html.

Stepaniak, Joanne. *Being Vegan: Living with Conscience, Conviction and Compassion*. Los Angeles, CA: Lowell House, 2000.

Tristram, Stuart. *The Bloodless Revolution: A Cultural History of Vegetarianism from 1600 to Modern Times*. New York, NY: W.W. Norton & Co., 2007.

Vegan Society, The. "Memorandum and Articles of Association." Retrieved November 12, 2017. https://www.vegansociety.com/about-us/history.

Vegetarian Times. "Vegetarianism in America, 2008." Retrieved November 12, 2017. https//www .vegetariantimes.com.

Watson, Donald. "The Vegan News." Issue 1. November 1944. https://issuu.com/vegan_society/docs /the_vegan_news_1944.

INDEX

ABOUT THE AUTHOR

Erica Green lives in New Zealand, where sheep are said to outnumber people. There is plenty of space for animals to feed on grass, yet New Zealand's dairy industry has grown so large in recent years that factory farming is now a reality. After researching this book, Green is now reconsidering her previous life as an omnivore.

PHOTO CREDITS

Cover Lucy von Held/Blend Images/Getty Images; p. 6 Wallace Kirkland/The LIFE Picture Collection/Getty Images; p. 8 Greg Doherty/Getty Images; p. 9 Pax Ahimsa Gethen/ Wikimedia Commons/Lauren Ornelas at UC Berkeley.jpg/ CC BY-SA 4.0; p. 12 veganninja/Wikimedia Commons/ Gary Yourofsky.jpg/CC BY-SA 4.0; p. 14 Angela Weiss/Getty Images; p. 19 AGF/Universal Images Group/Getty Images; p. 21 Sergey Gorshkov/Minden Pictures/Getty Images; p. 25 Enrique Diaz/7cero/Moment/Getty Images; p. 26 Westend61/ Getty Images; p. 29 The Washington Post/Getty Images; p. 31 William Shaw/Dorling Kindersley/Getty Images; p. 34 ilbusca/E+/Getty Images; p. 36 Africa Studio/Shutterstock .com; p. 37 elenabs/iStock/Thinkstock; p. 39 Photofusion/ Universal Images Group/Getty Images; p. 40 filadendron/E+/ Getty Images; p. 44 Sophie Ramis AFP/Newscom; p. 47 Jim Parkin/Shutterstock.com; p. 49 Bloomberg/Getty Images; p. 51 Jo-Anne McArthur/We Animals; back cover, interior pages background pattern (leaf) mexrix/Shutterstock.com; interior pages background pattern (bamboo) wow.subtropica/ Shutterstock.com.

Design and Layout: Tahara Anderson; Editor: Carolyn DeCarlo; Photo Researcher: Nicole Baker